A History of Mevagissey

Tales for the Red Lips

Liz Hurley

Mudlark's Press

Mudlark's Press

www.hurleybooks.co.uk

First Edition, 2017

ISBN: 9780993218026

A CIP catalogue record for this book is available from the British Library

Printed in Cornwall by TJ International

Cover design by Sally Mitchell

Typeset in Minion Pro and Avenir by Annabel Brandon

Image Copyright Fig. 2, 9, 13, 15, 19, 20. © Roly Deighton. Fig.14 © Bill Behenna. Fig.16, 17. © The National Trust.

CONTENTS

FOREWORD

This book could have been twenty times its current size, and maybe in future, it will be, but for now, it was commissioned to be a concise overview of Mevagissey's history. You may find that as you read a particular section that you want to know more. There is a further reading list in the back. You may be appalled that I didn't mention such and such a fact, trust me I have found the editing down process incredibly frustrating; there is so much fascinating stuff in Mevagissey's history. I hope that in this history you find something new or you get a desire to know more.

The book is comprised of primary and secondary sources, and I am indebted to Capt. Hugh Bowles, rt. Harbour Master, Bill Behenna, Roly Deighton, Mevagissey Museum and the Mevagissey Harbour Trust amongst others, for sharing their archives and their personal reminiscences with me. Any mistakes are of course all mine. In the meantime enjoy exploring Mevagissey through this history, and if you have any interesting facts or tales that you want to share with me, I would love to hear them.

TIMELINE

550 AD Saint Mevan is in the St Austell area.

1200s Heligan Manor built.

1259 Parish Church dedicated by Bishop Bronescombe.

1410 A stone pier (West Quay) was built on the northern side to protect the boats from easterlies.

1540 Described by the chronicler, John Leland, as a safe fishing harbour.

1753 John Wesley first visits. Methodism becomes very strong here.

1774 Act of Parliament allowed the quays to be enlarged (East and West Quay).

1808 Caerhays Castle built.

1824 Philip Ball & Son Bank collapses.

1849 Cholera outbreak.

1870 Mevagissey Post Office added to the Telegraph system.

1890 Streets lit by electricity, powered by the Mevagissey Electric Supply Company. Claimed to be the first in the UK.

1891 The newly erected outer harbour wall is washed away in a massive blizzard.

1922 New road "Valley Road" built.

NAMING OF MEVAGISSEY

Before we can even talk about the history of Mevagissey, I suppose we had better first discuss its name. Most visitors can't even pronounce it, MEGA-vissey anyone? The funny thing is though that Mevagissey doesn't even appear to be its real name. It could be a fifteenth-century fabrication.

The naming of Mevagissey is very convoluted, but it is also fascinating because the evolution of Mevagissey's name strikes at the very heart of the cultural clash between the Cornish and the English. There is no definitive explanation, but there are several theories.

Mevagissey is a settlement that grew from two separate habitations. The first was a fishing hamlet by the edge of the sea called Porthilly, mentioned in 1694. This was around the area we now know as East Wharf, Old Sands and Cliff Street. The second habitation was called Lammorek and was based around the Church, first mentioned in 1259.

Both Porthilly and Lammorek are believed to be Cornish words. Porthilly (porth meaning 'cove, harbour' and hyly meaning 'salt water, brine) and Lammorek meaning Church by the Sea (morek meaning maritime, and lan/lam being the old Cornish for Church.)

There are lots of spellings and mentions of Lammorek (Lamoreke, Lanvoreck, Lamorrec, Lamorek) and hardly any of Porthilly. Why the discrepancy? My suggestion is that no-one much cared about a small fishing hamlet, whereas a Church was a far more prominent place and was mentioned more frequently.

And in trying to delve back through the mists of time, we see a language declining and disintegrating. The Cornish language was not the language of the Church or of the State, and we have very few surviving pieces of work written in Cornish. Culturally, language was passed on orally, and everyone's interpretation of how to write those sounds down on paper was different. It was only as a language started to be codified and pinned down on paper that it began to gain stability and power. We can see spellings of English words constantly changing through the centuries, this is no doubt what was happening to Cornish but instead of strengthening and settling in print it began to unravel and disintegrate. I have found at least six different spellings of Lammorek with no consensus.

Now, something interesting happened in 1400; James Lamledyr referred to himself as vicar of 'Meffagesy', and this is the first recorded instance of Mevagissey in any spelling. From this point onward Mevagissey is now the standard description in all existing written documents. "Lammorek" is quietly discarded. (SEE FIG. 1.)

Once more we are back in the realm of speculation. Why the massive name change? Some historian suggests that as Lammorek and Porthilly began to merge, they needed a new name. However, that doesn't really hold water as what generally happens is that the weaker, poorer settlement just gets its name dropped.

Again, I believe this name change was down to the domination of the Church and the English language. Lammorek was Cornish, why not something spiritually uplifting? I would suggest that the Church decided to invent a history. The prevailing theory is that the name Mevagissey is the creation of two saints, named Meva and Issey. Why not? Cornwall was absolutely awash with Saints in the fifth century. There was a "flight path" from Ireland to Wales, through Cornwall and onto Brittany.

Given that there is no actual evidence for these saints we are working on conjecture again and the best guess is that it is named after St Mewan (also referred to as Maén and Mevan) and St Ita. Both contemporaries of each other around 550. We know St Mewan was in the area. There is no evidence that Saint Ita, a very famous Irish saint was in the area, but she was, according to some sources the aunt of St Petroc, and we know that he certainly had a massive impact on Cornwall. Maybe St Mevan wanted to honour St Petroc's aunt? Who knows, a more likely suggestion is that the Church, in the fifteenth century just picked two likely names, re-dedicated the church and created a new myth.

Either way, it seems more probable that for a long time there were several names. Orally, local people would probably have continued to refer to Porthilly and Lammorek but in writing the new Christian name would have been used in records and official documents. Visitors would be first introduced to the village through the written word , and so, due to the wider audience and the official versions, the Christian name grew in prominence.

Fig. 1. This is the oldest known image of Mevagissey and is still recognisable today.

However, as language twists and migrates over the centuries, you can see how the Church of St Mevan and St Ita went from that to Mevan "hag" Ita (hag is Cornish for and) and finally to Mevagissey. Or Meva, Mev or Mevie as we like to call it.

Just as a final sidebar, the Church is now called St Peter's. It seems that naming things in Mevagissey is a tricky thing to do.

RELIGION

Cornwall has always been deeply religious; just look at the number of Saints that Cornwall claims. The county is covered in shrines, holy wells and places of natural worship. Cornwall is awash with sites of pagan religion, stone circles, etc. As early Christianity took hold in Britain Cornwall embraced the new religion with fervour.

Life had always been hard but in Cornwall poverty was rampant, fishing and mining were hazardous occupations, the soil was often barren, and people were days from any large commercial centres. No wonder they turned to a higher power. It is unsurprising therefore that when the new religions of the Reformation began to emerge, the people of Cornwall took them up with a passion. These new religions spoke directly to the common man and focused on issues of poverty and Independence. The great Cornish religion is Methodism, a religion that was founded in the mid-1700s by John and Charles Wesley as a response to their dissatisfaction with the Church of England. Methodism spoke to the poor and downtrodden as it said that each person could talk to God directly, all were equal with no "princes" of the Church. Whilst it grew in popularity across the country, it was most vigorously taken up in Cornwall. John Wesley made around thirty-two trips to Cornwall when he was alive, and by the mid-nineteenth century it was the most popular religion in all of Cornwall; one of the few places in England where Methodism outstripped the Church of England. According to Wesley's journal, he visited Mevagissey on eight occasions, mentioning the place by name three times in his journal and in letters. Other accounts suggest he visited ten times, but whatever the actual figure is, it is clear that he enjoyed Mevagissey and was made welcome.

From the journals of John Wesley

Wednesday, August 8th, 1753. *First visit.* *"We were invited to Mevagissey, a small town on the south sea. As soon as we entered the town many ran together, crying, 'See, the Methodees are come.' But they only gaped and stared; so that we returned unmolested to the house I was to preach at, a mile from the town. Many serious people were waiting for us, but most of them deeply ignorant. While I was showing them the first principles of Christianity many of the rabble from the town came up. They looked as fierce as lions, but in a few minutes changed their countenance and stood still. Toward the close some began to laugh and talk, who grew more boisterous after I had concluded. But I walked straight through the midst of them, and took horse without any interruption."*

Thursday, September 22nd, 1757 *"I rode to Mevagissey, which lies on the south sea, just opposite to Port Isaac on the north. When I was here last, we had no place in the town; I could only preach about half a mile from it. But things are altered now: I preached just over the town, to almost all the inhabitants, and all were still as night. The next evening a drunken man made some noise behind me. But after a few words were spoken to him, he quietly listened to the rest of the discourse."*

Saturday, September 24th, 1757 *"At half-hour after twelve I preached once more and took my leave of them. All the time I stayed the wind blew from the sea so that no boat could stir out. By this means all the fishermen (who are the chief part of the town) had opportunity of hearing."*

Tuesday, August 13th, 1768 *"I preached in Truro and in the evening at Mevagissey. It was a season of solemn joy; I have not often found the like. Surely God's thoughts are not as our thoughts! Can any good be done at Mevagissey?"*

One of his early friendships in Mevagissey was with James Dunn. Local tradition has it that James Dunn was one of the fierce lions but following this lecture and the birth of his son James Dunn Jnr. the next year, James saw the light and a few years later (1757) personally invited Wesley back to address the village and made his own premises available. This is known as The Wheel House today. As the years progressed Wesley regularly visited Mevagissey and Dunn hosted him until his congregation became too large, and Dunn started to raise subscriptions for a meeting house. James Dunn continued to thrive, and it might be nice to think that this was down to his new found faith, but it probably had something to do with his continued smuggling career. In fact, when he built his new house on Fore Street he included hidden passages heading down to the quay, avoiding the Customs men waiting on Jetty Street. Once again the pragmatic nature of people struggling to thrive shines through. The friendship between Wesley and Dunn was well-known and was finally immortalised in a stained glass window in Truro Cathedral.

There is a final footnote on the friendship of Wesley and Dunn. Michael Morpurgo, the celebrated children's author came into Hurley Books and was chatting about his connection to the village; it turns out that he is a descendant of John Wesley. He then introduced me to his wife, Clare, who it turns out is a descendant of James Dunn. Three hundred years later their paths once more entwined.

GENERAL HISTORY

Despite the claims that Mevagissey is named after two sixth century saints, we don't have any evidence of the settlement until Church records in 1259 mention it as being re-consecrated by Bishop Bronescombe. It certainly doesn't appear in the Domesday records, but it was common for early Christian settlements to die out in the late Anglo-Saxon period. The reason for this is uncertain but widespread.

We have clear evidence for the prosperity of the village in the mid-seventeenth century, through a Mevagissey token. Tokens were popular in the seventeen-hundreds when the banks weren't able to keep up with currency demands. Frustrated, local businessmen began to mint their own coins, and we have one from 1664 stamped "John Keagle, fish merchant of Mibagyzey, 1664". (SEE FIG. 2.)

Mevagissey began to rise in fame in the Eighteenth century turning up in verse, and local records. Around the time of the new Harbour Trust, there was also talk of establishing Mevagissey as a Spa location. There was a Chalybeate well, known as Brass Well, on the Treleaven estate. This ran with pungent sulphurous waters, and local land owners thought that the site could be developed along the lines of Bath or Cheltenham. There is a Temple Woods, between the village and Heligan, so maybe plans got further than the drawing board? But beyond that, the Spa never materialised, and today, no sulphurous spring exists.

Fig. 2. Only two of these tokens are known to exist. The text on this token reads, "John Keagle, fish merchant of Mibagyzey, 1664."

In 1824 according to FWL Stockdale, *"Mevagizzy contains near 400 houses, and according to the late census, 2450 inhabitants. About two miles from the town, is Helegan, the seat Of the Rev. Henry Hawkins Tremayne, a very elegant and substantial residence, most beautifully situated and embellished with fine gardens and shrubberies, and When perfectly finished, will be as handsome a residence as any in the county."*

Despite the close proximity of neighbouring villages, rivalries often broke out. A well-established grudge existed between Mevagissey and Gorran, with both sides delighting in the folly of the other. In the words of Hitchen and Drew, 1824. (SEE FIG. 3.)

It has been said, that in former years the church of Mevagissey was graced with a tower, but on what authority this report is founded, is very dubious. The opinion, however, is still cherished in the memorials of tradition: and the following old doggerel rhymes, in which the inhabitants of Gorran are represented as upbraiding the natives of Mevagissey for their folly in demolishing their tower, are still repeated as commemorative of the fact.

Fig. 3. In this fine engraving for 1815 you can clearly see the absence of Middle Wharf

Ye men Of Porthilly,
Why were ye so silly,
In having so little a power;
You sold every bell,
As Gorran men tell,
For money to pull down your tower."

Whilst the Gorran men may have been laughing at the Mevagissey men it may well have been sour grapes prompted by a previous run-in. Again, in the words of Hitchen and Drew, 1824.

Many years since Mevagissey men finding fish on the Gorran coast went thither, and after some time one of their seans enclosed a considerable quantity. (A "sean" is the old spelling of seine, a type of large fishing net.) Having secured their net with grapnels, they returned home, leaving their sean in the water. Nearly about the same time a sean from Gorran enclosed another shoal not far from the spot in which the Mevagissey sean lay and having secured their net they also retired. Finding however that the way was clear, Gorran men went out in the night, and repaired to the spot in which they knew the Mevagissey sean to be secured, and under cover of darkness, they took it out of the water, cut it in pieces, and turned away the fish; encouraging each other while thus engaged, with these words "cut away, it is a Mevagissey sean." Just as they had finished their nefarious work, and thrown the fragments overboard, Mevagissey boats arrived ; but instead of going to these mutilated remnants of the sean, they went to the other which still retained its fish, which they actually found to be their own, the tide having driven this from its original spot, and carried that of Gorran into its place. On making this discovery Gorran men were much alarmed; and from further observations, they were mortified to learn that, they had actually destroyed their own sean , and turned away their own fish! This tale is still bandied about among the fishermen when their boats happen to meet in the Bay.

The success of Mevagissey's fishing industry began to outstrip the village's ability to cope with it, and many commentated on the narrowness of the streets and the filth and fish guts lying in the open.

The streets of Mevagissey are in general exceedingly narrow, and in some parts, their intricacy and unexpected turnings surpass even the scantiness of their contracted dimensions. On this account the Pilchards, during the season, are invariably carried by men instead Of horses, in large maunds; through the handles of which a pole passes, which rests on their shoulders. As a natural consequence of their narrowness, the streets Of Mevagissey are frequently dirty, and they may be fairly contrasted with the abodes of the inhabitants; which from time immemorial have been proverbial for cleanliness, without excepting the humble cottages of the fishermen.

Despite the cleanliness of the locals they were horribly struck down by cholera only a few decades later.

The Illustrated London News. August 25th, 1849 "Cholera at Mevagissey"

This town has been fearfully visited by the cholera; the number of deaths from the first breaking out of the disease to the 15th instant being 111 in a population never exceeding 1800 and reduced, the first week after the appearance of the disease, through people leaving the town, to about 1000 or 1200. We learn from the West Briton that the most active sanitary measures have been carried into effect. Ordnance tents have been brought down capable of holding four or five hundred persons, and have been erected at Port Mellon, on the side of a hill; and in these tents, on Wednesday the 15th, about two hundred of the people of Mevagissey were located. The fish cellars at Port Mellon are also occupied having been divided into compartments with canvas under the direction of Mr Bowie, the Government Inspector from the General Board of Health. A corps of scavengers is established, and the sluice is fitted at the bottom of the river so as to flush the water through the greater part of the town and cleanse the filth. So many people have left and so disastrous has been the calamity that the town now does not now contain more than five or six hundred persons. Under the advice of the medical officers, it is determined that no party shall be worked about the fishery more than eight hours in the

CHOLERA AT MEVAGISSEY, IN CORNWALL.—ENCAMPMENT OF THE INHABITANTS AT PORT MELLON.—(SEE NEXT PAGE.)

Fig.4. Image of Portmellon in 1849. the tents on the hill were erected to house the residents of Mevagissey as they tried to escape the outbreak.

twenty-four, so that disease should not be brought on by fatigue; also that
every attention shall be paid to the food and comfort of those employed; and
that the whole of the fish brought on shore shall at once be placed in bulk
without being gutted so as to produce as little filth as possible.

In the Sketch which with which we have been favoured by correspondence
at Mevagissey a refers to Mr Kendall's cellars; b, other cellars; c, hospital
recently and inn; d, cellars; e, encampment ordnance tents; f,g,h, occupied
by refugees; i, the Bay of Mevagissey. (SEE FIG. 4.)

A visual reminder of the numbers involved can be seen in the village graveyard.
A tombstone for Peter Furse, who died from cholera, stands on its own. The
land surroundING his stone was a mass pit for the dead who were too poor
to mark their own burial site. In two months the village lost nearly 6% of its
population. Despite this savage blow to the community, Mevagissey soon
restored itself, primarily through the profits brought by the fishing industry.

MEVAGISSEY AT WAR

Mevagissey has been lucky enough to avoid the worst of warfare but war has
still left its mark, and for some, it has proved life-changing.

Being a seaport, Mevagissey must have been continually involved in
providing able seaman for the Navy, and many of our Master Mariners did
their duty. According to Hitchens and Drew, writing in 1824, a battery of six,
eighteen-pounder guns along the eastern edge of the village, was erected about
the commencement of the American war in 1775. However, they were never
called into use, nor were they during the following, Napoleonic conflict. Their
location is now marked by the naming of "Battery Terrace", but other clues
remain. If you look closely around Old Sands, near the Harbour Master's Office,
you may notice some odd bollards where the boats tie up. These are what are
left of the guns. Fishermen will recycle 'til the Cod come home. (SEE FIG. 5.)

Mevagissey was again embroiled in the First World War in a way that eighty years later was going to draw the world's attention to it. As the call went out for soldiers to fight, many of the local men and boys signed up, including many of the farm hands and gardeners from Heligan. Sailors joined the Navy; land boys joined the Army. The First World War almost wiped out a generation of young men and the Heligan estate, bereft of staff, fell into decline. Only six of the twenty-two staff who signed up, returned. Gradually the beautiful gardens were lost under weeds and trees; greenhouses fell in, paths were lost, pavilions grown over. The family moved out of the house and decay set in. During the Eighties to much fanfare and excitement, it was "re-discovered", and a restoration project began that drew the attention of the world. The Lost Gardens of Heligan now employs 88 full-time members of staff, with this number swelling to over 130 staff during summer. They have won countless awards, regularly winning the UK's favourite garden and have been visited and enjoyed by over five million people.

Fig.5. All that remains of the eighteen-pounder guns, erected about the commencement of the American war in 1775. This one can be found near the Harbour Master's office.

Of course, the locals smile at this, 'Ligan was never lost. Children grew up playing in its wilds, exploring the hidden paths, scrumping from the neglected orchards and generally having a lot of fun in their own private fantasy gardens. They even explored it during school trips.

The First World War was a strange time of contrasts. From the horror of the trenches to the manners of the sea. On the 27th of November 1917, the SS Eastfield was in the sights of UB-57, and the cargo vessel didn't stand a chance. UB-57 was commanded by Kapitan Otto Steinbrinck, who in the past month had sunk ten boats and would add a further forty-six boats in the year to come. The SS Eastfield was hit a few miles outside of Mevagissey. The lifeboat, the James Chisholm, was launched and dashed out to see if aid could be offered. The men in the boat rowed out knowing that there was a U-Boat in the water but when they got to the stricken ship, they found the U-Boat above the surface and Steinbrinck observing the scene. He allowed all the crew to be rescued and gave the lifeboat safe passage back to Mevagissey. The Eastfield still sits 50m below on the sea floor, its cargo of coal scattered across the seabed. Site location 50°14.255'N 4°42.262'W

The Second World War was once again a chance for Mevagissey to help stock the nation's larder and feed those on rations. Mevagissey, so far away from the blitzed cities became a refuge for their children and many fondly remember coming from bombed cities to a village surrounded by the sea and fields. Maybe they too explored Heligan whilst they waited to return to their families? The Mevagissey area wasn't completely unaffected though. Here are the words of John Chiswell, a seven-year-old evacuee who witnessed an attack, whilst living in the neighbouring village of Pentewan.

> *"For me, life in Pentewan was idyllic after being in 'The Plymouth Blitz'.*
> *We were able to play in the open with no fear of any more bombs. That is*
> *until one day in August 1942 when I was playing outside Westcliffe - to my*
> *amazement a low flying plane came in from the direction of what is now*
> *the campsite. The plane was so low as it flew over me that I can vividly*
> *remember the pilot in his headgear and goggles looking down at me. It*
> *is now a matter of history that he dropped his bombs and the Methodist*
> *Chapel was destroyed. It was only a short time before that I had been*

walking down North Row past the chapel with some other children after playing out towards the woods – clearly someone was looking after us!

My memory is so clear on the events of that day – I remember Miss Stedman kneeling down in the road to pray. The chapel was the emergency food store for the village; North Row was littered with cans of food. The large pipes of the chapel organ were scattered around in the debris and, as youngsters, we had great fun trying to blow them to make some sound. The village was a mess. The devastation was nothing like I had seen in Plymouth but, for our wonderful village life, this was a whole new chapter."

The village continues to be involved in conflicts as its population go off and serve in the armed forces. Thankfully few names have been added to our war memorial, but it was with great sadness that Sapper Elijah Bond died in Helman Province in 2011 and his name joined the sorrowful list.

MINING

Whilst much of Cornwall is famed for its mining it's not something that springs to mind when you think about Mevagissey, but we did once have our very own mine right on the harbour. Wheal Kendall didn't last long though, and it's fair to say that there must have been more money in fishing. The mine was heavily backed by Ball's Bank, Mevagissey's own bank that was so prosperous it even produced its own bank notes.

However, in 1824, the bank failed which had a significant impact on many industries and personal worth for many in the area including St Austell, where the China Clay industry also had an interest. The mine collapsed but I suspect that if there was money to be had from Wheal Kendall, it would have survived the bank crash. There are other small lodes and deposits of antimony, copper, tin and nickel within a five-mile radius but these seams, like the Mevagissey copper mine, petered away and appeared not to have been worth the effort.

Mines and Miners of Cornwall. xiii The Lizard - Falmouth - Mevagissey. AJ Hamilton Jenkin 1967.

Of mining proper Mevagissey has also witnessed its small share. Among these was WHEAL KENDALL which according to a notice in the West Briton, 26th September 1828, was then for sale to the highest bidder - "tenders to be with by Mr William Francis, Gwennap, Churchtown" It would seem that most of the shareholders hailed from that great copper mining parish, and from this one may infer that Wheal Kendall itself was probably a trial for copper. That the Gwennap men in this instance were far from being a happy band of brothers is shown by another notice which appeared a few months later in the same newspaper: "A certain party on that said mine (Wheal Kendall) holding about one-fourth part, having sought proper to work the said mine, and to contract debts thereon contrary to the usual custom of mining, I, Hercules Michell, representing a majority of the shareholders in the above mine do you protest against such proceedings and do not hold myself liable after this public notice for any debts made or contracted by William Francis or Samuel Pollard, now working the said mine, Gwennap 14th January 1829."

The "mine," according to the late Mr Frank Baron of Mevagissey in a letter to the writer of 6th May 1958, consisted of a large adit driven in at high-water mark beneath the wooden bridge which formally spanned a gap in the cliff on Polkirt Hill leading towards Portmellon. From here the adit extended under the fields of Churchpark Farm (O.S. 59 S.E.) which being long tenanted by the Kendall family, no doubt gave the adventure its name. The entrance to the adit was blocked when the bridge was removed and the present sea-wall built. It now lies buried some forty feet below the roadway. (SEE FIG. 6.)

In December 1775 and application was with received to make trials for copper on the Treleaven estate, some three-quarters of a mile to the north-west of Mevagissey. Although the position of the sett was not clearly defined it undoubtedly

Fig.6. This is the only known image of Wheal Kendall from 1825. This side of the village has changed dramatically. Use the flight of steps to help navigate, as they are still present today. The little men on the bridge are standing on Polkirt Hill, the building to the left by the water is very roughly where West Wharf loos are today.

comprised the valley bottom lying between the Treleaven Plantation and Temple Wood (O.S. 59 S.E.). Here there formally existed a spring of chalybeate water known to the country people as Brass Well from the sulphurous scum which floated on its surface, and highly regarded for its curative properties in the days when the cleanliness came a poor second to godliness. In 1836 a company named Wheal Brass Well carried out further investigations near this spot. Two adits, the portals of which can still (1959) be traced, were extended beneath the Treleaven Plantation, whilst nearly opposite these, a like number are said to have been driven into the steep slopes of Temple Wood. The site of these operations now lies in a bog and a dense thicket of brambles which made their examination by the writer and his friend Geoffrey Ordish one of the most arduous of the many excursions they have undertaken together "in the fields."

HARBOUR

The earliest evidence we have for the harbour is around 1550 when a stone quay was built in the general location of the existing East Quay, jutting out from the Harbour Masters office towards West Quay. The area known as Old Sand, the beach in front of the museum and boat yard, is clearly where the fishing village began. The rocks behind, providing a level of protection that was then reinforced by the medieval harbour wall. This section of the harbour is known as Island Quay, and you can see in old paintings that the buildings were once accessed via a bridge. Each fisherman ran his own business, and no boat owner operated a fleet of vessels. There was no collective or dominant voice, and so it was the land owners that profited from the overall fishing industry; they clubbed together to establish and run a better infrastructure than currently existed. 1774 marked the first meeting of the Mevagissey Harbour Trust and was held in the Ship Inn. The Harbour Trust is a charity that exists to protect and promote all users and uses of the harbour; tourists, sailors, traders and fishermen all have an equal footing. The records for these first meetings still

Fig.7. This dramatic image from 1825 shows boats running for shelter ahead of an easterly wind. Old Sand is separate from East Wharf, and there is no outer harbour.

exist in the Harbour offices. Whilst most official ledgers are bound in cow leather, this set of documents are bound in Ling, a member of the Cod family, a rare but appropriate binding and one in plentiful supply in Mevagissey. Fish leather is five times stronger than that of cow, so maybe we could have started a new industry in book bindings? During this period the eastern harbour wall was strengthened, and the West Quay (where the fish store now sits) was built along with the jetty and wharves running along the front of the harbour. East and West Quay enclose the inner harbour. (SEE FIG. 7.)

In a relatively short period of time, Mevagissey was recognised for the port that it had become and was viewed as an important location for coastal trade by Parliament. We can see from the tariff roll for the landing of goods how prosperous the harbour was. Goods included tin, wine, tobacco, stone, figs, cider ropes, varnish, hemp, flour, earthenware and so on. (SEE FIG. 8.)

Mevagissey was clearly a prosperous and well-known port, but its primary industry was about to emerge. The rise of the fishing industry and of one particular fish, the pilchard, catapulted Mevagissey into national and European fame.

In 1886 an Act was passed enabling the construction of the Outer Harbour, this was duly built and then washed away at vast expense on March 11th, 1891

Fig.8. 1892. The Snowflake, a topsail schooner alongside the jetty where she was a regular sight. Watching her manoeuvring in and out must have been quite a thing.

during a rare blizzard. To destroy a newly-constructed harbour either says a lot about the construction of the harbour or the ferocity of the storm. Indeed this blizzard was a remarkable event. For five days the blizzard battered the south of England. Large areas of Cornwall were left under snowdrifts between eight and fifteen foot high. Villages were cut off for weeks, ships were thrown onto rocks, and much property was destroyed. It is estimated that 200 people died and 6000 livestock. In The Gazette, the UK's Official Public Record, the destruction of the Mevagissey pier and ability to man the lighthouse, was not announced until April 14th, almost a month later. Given the severity of the loss, it shows that it took a very long time to get the message to London. The country had come to a standstill. As Mevagissey is surrounded by steep hills, I imagine the villagers were cut off for days.

The pier was rebuilt, and by 1895 the lighthouse was one of the first in the country to be powered by electricity. North Pier completed in 1897 and Victoria Pier now protected the outer harbour known as The Pool. The beach to the right of West Quay is known as Sandy Beach. Like all the beaches around the harbour, it is submerged at high tide. Also in 1895, Middle Wharf was built up to connect the jetty to West Wharf. Prior to this, the sea came right up to the buildings' walls.

In 1869 a lifeboat station was built but only ran until 1930. It was prone to storm damage and eventually closed. During its short lifespan though it was home to three successive boats; the South Warwickshire, the John Arthur and the James Chisholm. In all, fifty-eight souls were saved during their sixty years of service. Before and after that, lifeboat cover was provided by Fowey. The lifeboat station now provides a home for the Mevagissey Aquarium, run by the Harbour Trust and funded by donations. The outer harbour wall has many benefits; it creates a greater degree of calm in the inner harbour, it provides more sheltered anchorage in deeper water, and it offers more storage and wharf side space. The jetty was extended in 2015 in order to give additional space for dry dock repairs and a second crane has also been recently installed.

Storm damage continues to be a severe threat to our east facing harbour and the inner and outer harbour walls offer incredible protection. The following photos show what happens to properties outside the safety of these walls. (SEE FIG. 9.)

Fig.9. This house was built just to the left of the Watch House and not benefiting from the harbour walls. You can see that there was a single flat wall. For all the good it did. The owners had just bought this house the day before the storm.

The Harbour Trust have always planned ahead and re-invested in their land, and one of the less well-known facts was in purchasing the fundus (the sea floor) from the Duchy in 1888. This gives the Harbour Trust complete control over their land, and they are one of the few harbours in the UK to own their own fundus. A more controversial act was the removal of the bins from the harbour side. The Harbour Trust owns all the land from the wharves out to the piers, and so this is not Council or Highways property. The Trust was having to pay the Council to remove the rubbish, and this was totalling £26K a year. As a charity, they decided that this was not a good use of their money and so the bins were removed, to much hue and cry. However, everyone has now become used to the idea, there are Council bins within the village, and if people are made to think about packaging and waste, then this can only be a good thing. All food retailers are happy to take back any packaging and recycling levels in Mevagissey, have no doubt risen.

FISHING

Nature has always dictated that Mevagissey would be good for fishing. The land is shaped into a small cove leading quickly into deep water. The bay faces East which is excellent given that the prevailing wind is South West and the sea has always been bountiful. The village has always been referred to as a fishing village in historical records, and it is clear that the birth and growth of Mevagissey was purely down to fishing.

The main catch was pilchards. For reasons that are unclear the pilchard began to turn up in our waters in vast numbers. The whole of the St Austell Bay benefited from this bounty, but it was Mevagissey that was pre-eminent in the fishing industry. Although not particularly popular in Britain, the pilchard was highly sought after on the continent. At one point in the early 1900's, the St Austell Bay area exported around 75 million pilchards. (SEE FIG. 10.)

To process the fish, they were first salted in brine tanks and then packaged in wooden casks. The casks had holes in the bottom, and a lid was placed on top to which weights were added in order to squeeze the oil from the fish. To further leverage the squeeze, a long pole was slotted into the hole in the wall, and weights were tied to the end of it. The pole rested on top of the lid and pressed the pilchard. The lids were then fitted, and the barrels were shipped out. Many buildings in the village were used for this process. Very few signs of these presses exist today; some are hidden behinds protective walls, others are features in private homes. However, one set of press holes can still be viewed in an old wall in a private car park by the Model Railway Museum. (SEE FIG. 11.)

You may be forgiven for thinking that the holes that you can see along the top of East Quay are press holes. However, I have been reliably informed by Malcolm Solomon that these are the remnants of a movie set, *Next of Kin*, and were gun emplacements.

The rise in pilchard popularity was two-fold. As a fish in vast quantity, it was much appreciated by the largely Catholic Europeans who could only eat

Fig.10. Here you can see the catch being made ready for market or pressing on the Jetty. Pawlyn's were a Mevagissey fish merchant. You can see their name on two of the barrels.

fish on certain days of the week. The second benefit was the oil that could be squeezed out of it. This oil was flammable and provided reliable street lighting, a century before electricity. It was mentioned in the following poem by Peter Pindar in 1775;

Hail Mevagizzy! What a town of note!
Where boats, and men, and stinks, and trade are stirring;
Where pilchards come in myriads to be caught:
Pilchard! A thousand times as good's herring.
Pilchard! The idol of the Popish nation!
Hail, little instrument of vast-salvation!

Fig.11. A pilchard press in action. The pilchards were arranged in layers; a weighted lid was put on top. Then a long pole was fitted into the wall slot and placed on top of the barrel cover. Further weights were tied to the end of the pole to add further pressure.

Pilchard, I ween, the most soul-saving fish,
On which the Catholics in Lent are crammed;
Who, had they not, poor souls, this lucky dish,
Would flesh eat, and be consequently damned.
Pilchards! whose bodies yield the fragrant oil,
And makes the London lamps at midnight smile;
Which lamps, wide spreading salutary light,
Beam on the Wandering Beauties of the night,
And show each gentle youth their cheeks' deep roses,
And tell him, whether they have eyes and noses.

The "beauties of the night" were clearly prostitutes and the reference to eyes and noses was clearly alluding to syphilis. So there we were, helping out punters and the Pope alike, back in the 1700s. No wonder pilchards were so popular.

The seas around Mevagissey had always been rich with a diverse range of fish; pollack, ling, cod, whiting, eel, hake, mullet, bream, gurnard, dogfish, porbeagle, rays, monk, plaice, turbot, brill, lemon sole, dover sole, john dory, anchovies, mackerel, pilchards, herrings, sand eels, wrasse, cuttlefish, octopus, squid, spider crab, brown crab, lobster and crayfish. And of course, this is just the edible catch. Our seas are also home to sharks, dolphins and whales. Recently a family of humpback whales have been seen off the Cornish south coast. In the past, there were also frequent mentions of grampus, an old word for orcas or killer whales. No doubt they were here for the giant shoals of pilchards. The days of giant shoals though have gone; they began to dry up in the early part of the twentieth century. It is thought that the larger commercial boats that could go out further to sea and catch more contributed to the declining numbers. Others believe that it may have been a change in sea currents. Either way, the orcas and pilchards are now gone. (SEE FIG. 12.)

During the Fifties and Sixties, the fishing industry began to decline, and Mevagissey seemed destined to become just a tourist destination, but the Eighties began to see a regrowth thanks to large mackerel landings. The Harbour Trust continued to invest in the fishing industry with help from UK and EU funds, and in 1993 the value of fish landings was £963,120. In 2014 it had grown to over £2 million, making Mevagissey the second most prosperous harbour in Cornwall, after Newlyn. The industry is growing, as can also be seen in the

Fig.12. A Mevagissey fisherman tending to his lines and his maund basket. Jack Dunn, in his book "Memories of Mevagissey" transcribed by Archie Smith, said that this was pronounced as "mooan".

average age of the crew. More and more younger men are joining the industry, but it remains a dangerous and insecure one. If the boats can't get out due to weather no one gets paid, injuries are common, and deaths still occur. Boats sink and catches dry up. For all the apparent romance of the fisherman's life, it remains a perilous one. Only a few years ago one of our fishing boats sank at sea, and Ian Thomas, better known as Ginge, died, a memorial stone in his honour sits by the jetty. Events like this rock a small fishing village and whilst everyone helps and supports there is still more support that the families need. Our two most popular charities are the RNLI and the Fisherman's Mission, a charity that helps out fishermen and their families in any way they require; spiritual, emotional or financial.

SMUGGLING

It's easy to think of smuggling as an illegal activity, but what needs to be understood right from the outset is that it resulted directly from a Government trying to raise funds. Merchants and traders suddenly found themselves having taxes imposed on them. For people living on the edge and seeing no benefit from these taxes they unsurprisingly chose not to pay. For generations, they had traded without interference and knew their business inside out. Over the years, as the government tightened their system, merchants either began to pay or learnt to wear two hats and of course, some dropped the legal side of their business altogether. Smuggling did lead to wreckers and violence, but for many, it started and remained a way to avoid paying onerous taxes to up-country fat cats, as they would have been viewed at the time. (SEE FIG. 13.)

Mevagissey is riddled with secret passageways, tiny alleyways, hidden cellars, concealed doorways and doorways in rooftops. Walk up around the little lanes and ops above the east wharf, and you step back 300 years with each step you take. Incidentally, an Op or ope is a Cornish term for small alleyway or passage. See if you can find the wonderfully named Shilly Alley Op, you'll be rewarded with an excellent pint if you do.

Fig.13. Cliff Street and its associated little alleyways give a sense of what life was like. This photo is from the late 1800s and looks identical today. Ella Barbery is sitting on the step with her mother, Mary Jane Langford Pearce. With thanks to Roly Deighton for this photo and identification, Ella is his Grandmother. The man and children are unknown.

It's easy to see how things came off the boats and then vanished away in the night with nothing for the Customs men to tax.

THE RIVER BACK

Given the topography of Mevagissey, sitting at the bottom of a steep valley beside the sea, it is not surprising that we should have a river but not many notice it, as for the most part it remains hidden, either underground or hidden behind buildings. The River Back skirts along the path leading towards Heligan and then alongside the park. It flows under the road by Willow Car Park. In the past the river ran through this marshy field, populated with willows. The river can then be seen again running behind Chapel Street; Chapel Street used to be referred to as Back Lit.

The meaning of "Lit" is unclear, "letch" is an old term for a stream flowing through boggy ground, so maybe it's a historic corruption? It could mean "leat" but there was already a leat in Mevagissey, and it wasn't here.

The river's final appearance is through the grills on the road outside the leather shop where it finally flows into the harbour. There are clues to its historic open air path; the River Street Cafe in Market Square is one clue as is the fact that Market Square used to be known as Town Bridge. For most of the year, the river flows underground and unnoticed until we get heavy rains when it makes its presence felt. Sometimes this is a little flooding at the Willow Valley car park, its natural flood plain, sometimes during prolonged heavy rainfall, it turns the harbour waters an opaque orange-brown colour as it deposits the runoff from the fields above the village. Due to the river's small size, the catchment only 4.9 km² in area, and the river itself is only three km in length; it rarely contributes to severe flooding.

On old maps, we can see that the river was once split and that a leat was created to power a waterwheel located where the RNLI and surrounding shops sit. This wheel powered the village flour mill. The location of the mill pond

Fig.14. This is the only known image in existence of the overshot waterwheel taken in 1875. It was powered by a leat that had been syphoned off the river near where the football pitch sits today. Where the man is standing is roughly the corner between Moore's Grocery and the Lifeboat shop.

where the leat was hived off looks to have been where the football pitch now sits. This mill was still running in 1906, but no photos remain, and today there is no trace of the leat or mill other than in place names such as Leatfield, River Street and Mill House. (SEE FIG. 14.)

FLOODING

Mevagissey's other obvious source of water is the sea. During particularly high spring tides the harbour front can get a little wet as the sea climbs higher than the surrounding road. For this to occur a variety of factors need to combine. Firstly, you need a high tide, and then any of the following factors play a role; saturated fields, heavy rainfall, a strong easterly wind blowing straight into the mouth of the village funnelling waves towards the harbour, or a depression in the weather allowing the surface level of the sea to rise by many centimetres. The earth's atmosphere is measured by pressure. High pressure makes the air denser which pushes down the surface of the water. Low pressure makes the air less dense or "heavy" and allows the sea to expand or rise up. One centimetre may not sound a lot but think about the volume of an extra centimetre stretched all across the sea surface being funnelled by wind and waves towards the village.

These factors are relatively common, and you will see the sea creep in over the jetty and around the edges of the harbour quite often. Occasionally Market Square will also flood; despite the square not being by the sea front, it is actually lower than streets that are closer to the sea, such as Jetty Street or Fore Street and of course it has a river running under it. Water is a great leveller, and during a mild flood, you can see which streets are higher and which are lower. It's also a good time to spot the original builders of the village at work. Jetty Street funnels east and would make a perfect channel for the sea to continue to rise in and flood the village, but when it was built, it was constructed with a deliberate hump. It is not instantly noticeable, but it's there and very efficient in stopping flood water. The other thing to bear in mind with a tidal flood is that after an

Fig.15. Portmellon is a half mile south of us and faces in exactly the same direction.
Without harbour walls, there is nothing to stop an easterly storm.

hour or so it recedes as the tide does. These small floods are regular events and rarely cause so much as a twitch of an eyebrow. Shopkeepers sandbag their doorways (spring high tides occurring around 6 am and 6 pm in our part of the world.) Children giggle splashing around in the giant puddle and life goes on.

Occasionally, however, everything comes together; heavy rains, saturated fields, a river in spate, a spring high tide, a very low depression and a strong easterly and the village faces a severe flood. This happened most noticeably at the turn of the last century and again most recently in 2010. Once again boats were seen in Market Square, and many householders were flooded out of their homes and weren't able to return for many months. It was a long and challenging time for the village, but again it recovered. The builders of Mevagissey should be praised for their skilled works during this massive flood as Jetty Street remained dry at its highest point. As desired by the original builders, the sea and the river were not able to join forces at this point. This helped protect the top end of Fore Street.

Storm damage is also an issue but we are fortunate to shelter behind harbour walls. The following photos show what happens without the safety of these walls. Portmellon, our neighbour, suffered this damage in the sixties and is regularly drenched in huge waves. (SEE FIG. 15.)

PUBS

The beating heart of most villages is the pub although, in Cornwall, where Methodism was the dominant religion and one that advocated temperance, this is less true than in other parts of Britain. One area of Cornwall that clung resolutely to its pubs though was the Cornish fishing villages, and Mevagissey had ten! The old adage, a drinking village with a fishing problem, certainly applies to Meva. This wonderful poem by Frank Baron lists them all. See if can work out exactly where they used to stand.

Mevagissey Pubs

While Mevagissey stalwarts toiled
When George-the-Third was king
They needed oft refreshment
And constant strengthening.
Ten inns provided stimulant,
Termed taverns at the first,
And home-brewed beer flowed copiously
To slake perpetual thirst.

Five of the inns were spacious,
The other five were small,
THE FOUNTAIN by 'Shill-alley-opp'
Was father of them all;
By old Porthilly fishermen
Its threshold was well worn
When Mevagissey's straggling streets
Had not, as yet, been born.

Long years before the harbour changed
From creek into a port
THE CUTTER Inn stood on the cliff,
The jowters' chief resort.
Each hooker, on the cliffside's edge
Spread out his fish for sale,
And sold his catch ere he lifted the latch
For a pint of the Cutters sale.

Then, later, as the little town
Sprang from its mud-flat bed,
The KING'S ARMS hung its swinging sign

Close to the jetty head.
This tavern by the water side
Was, by unhappy fate,
Burnt down one Monday afternoon
In Eighteen-fifty-eight.

It lay in ruin, bleak and black,
Some few short years until
A new Kings Arms served patrons
At the foot of Polkirt Hill.
The SHIP INN laid her moorings down
On limpet shells and slime,
Cob-walled, straw-thatched and whitewashed
In Oliver Cromwell's time.

The ship, rebuilt in later years,
Acquired new dignity,
Front parlour for the gentlemen,
Ship captains home from sea,
And men of rank who proudly drank
Brandy, not common beer,
The lesser fry could occupy
The kitchen at the rear.

The LION INN adjoined the ship,
And oft the lion's roar
Disturbed the peaceful atmosphere
Of the genteel inn next door,
When, from the Lion's dim-let den,
Piercing the party wall,
The seiners sang with the smuggling gang,
Coopers and cobblers all.

Fish-jowters bellowed loud and long,
The fishwives sharp and shrill,
From lungs of leather rose and song
Louder and louder still.
When ` The Farmer Boy ` was ended
The crowd struck up anew
` Health to the Barley Moo,' me lads,
Health to the Barley Moo.

Amanda Snell's thatched Kiddlywink
Has long since passed away,
Lloyd's Bank now occupies the site,
And right across the way
The LONDON INN displayed its sign,
Welcoming travellers in
To sample good old Roscoff Rum
Or noggin of smuggled in.

Further along the cobbled street
(Post-office afterward)
The GLOBE INN'S ever open door
Led to Its wide back-yard,
Where frequent auction sales were held
In pipe-smoke thick as fog,
With many a bickering over bids
And many a glass of grog.

The RING-O-BELLS was in Jetty Street,
By the slip to the western quay,
Next door, the CROWN AND ANCHOR Inn
Was famed for minstrelsy.
Each Feasten Week its jovial bar
Kept humming like a hive

When ` Emmidy' the fiddler came
To keep the dance alive.

The HOPE INN, next door to the Crown,
Took in the overflow,
Three pubs in Jetty Street alone,
While stragglers had to go
To find their frothing pewter pints
In yet two thirst-quellers.
One kiddlywink by the old mill wheel
Another near Gould's cellars.

Low tide would leave the harbour dry,
Flood tide surged up ` back revver,'
If mill-pool dropped, the mill-wheel stopped,
But the beer flowed constant ever.

Sadly these days we are down to seven but three of those mentioned still stand. The Fountain Inn remains the father of them all and the King's Arms despite its fire and change of location, continues to thrive. The Ship Inn remains in the centre of the village. Our pubs today, as well as the three just mentioned are the Sharksfin, Harbour Tavern, Cellar Bar and of course the Mevagissey Social Club. To this day they remain at the heart of village life; not only do they feed and water us, but they also provide entertainment, support Feast Week and the Christmas lights. They are at the centre of most fundraising events and keep us warm and merry during the long winter months. Long may they continue to do so.

CELEBRATIONS & VILLAGE LIFE

Feast Week

A Cornish feast was a time to rest, celebrate and offer up thanks. Mevagissey's feast day was first recorded in 1754. It is celebrated around June 29th, the saint day of St Peter, for whom the church had been re-named. This makes it one of the oldest recorded festivals in Cornwall, and over the years we have managed to extend it to a full week of celebrations.

Christmas Lights

A more recent pair of celebration has been the Whitsun celebrations to raise funds for the Christmas Lights. At the end of May, there is a great fundraiser with live music and stall raising money for the lights. On the first Saturday of December, there is a lantern procession through the streets, and then the lights are switched on.

Over the past few years, there have been a range of advent activities, carols, storytelling, craft events, etc., taking part all across the village in various locations, including people's front rooms.

Mevagissey Male Choir

Many of these occasions will be graced by the talents of our local choir. Founded in 1974, the Mevagissey Male Choir first practised in Gary Mitchell's boatshed. They have performed in Westminster Abbey, three times, as well as the Royal Albert Hall, and across the States and Europe. Throughout summer they give free, evening concerts, on the jetty in Mevagissey. In Whitsun, there is a service for the Fishermen's Mission Blessing of the Fleet on The Jetty. The Choir perform following the blessing, and it is a wonderful open-air, community event.

Mevagissey Gig Club

Mevagissey Rowing Club is one of the oldest in Cornwall, established in 1987. They are the proud owners of three beautiful pilot gigs: Elowen, Lannvorek and Endeavour. Based at Portmellon, just a mile from Mevagissey, they row in the evenings throughout the summer, and at weekends during the winter.

MEVAGISSEY CHARACTERS

Andrew Pears

Andrew was born on his father's farm near Mevagissey. In 1789 he moved to London where he trained to be a barber, later opening a barber's shop in Gerrard Street, Soho. His upper-class clients had a delicate white complexion that needed a gentle soap. He found a way of removing the impurities and refining the base soap to produce a high-quality product that had the additional benefit of being transparent. His method of mellowing and ageing each long lasting Pears Bar, for over two months, is still used today. Andrew Pears retired from business in 1838, leaving his grandson, Francis, to continue the business of the London-based firm of A & F Pears. Andrew died in London in 1845. Pears Soap was the world's first registered brand and is, therefore, the world's oldest continuously existing brand.

Angelo John Calicchia

The name may not at first seem familiar, but that's because as a young man Angelo's father decided that as an Italian immigrant he stood out too much in Cornwall and changed his name to Kelly. He made ice cream.

Angelo's parents came over to Cornwall and settled in St Austell; his father was a hard man who made his children earn their keep as soon as they were able. School was very much an afterthought. Angelo remembers as a lad in the thirties going door-to-door selling apples and turnips. He would go to a farmer and buy a tree-load or two strips of the field and then take the harvest to sell on his weekly rounds in the local villages. He would sell apples by the quarter and turnips (swedes) by size. Half a small turnip was a farthing. He remembers when no one would come to the door to buy a farthing's worth of food that those behind the door were probably cold and hungry. A familiar sight was children scraping their nail along the *crick* of the pilchard barrels to get some oil to eat. Poverty was a genuine issue, and local doctors remember as late as the Sixties helping patients dealing with the pain of overeating on a pilchard glut.

Angelo grew up with the immigrant spirit for working hard every hour, and gradually he built up an ice cream business. He had strong memories of Mevagissey, and when wharf side properties were offered to him, he bought them and opened ice cream parlours. At one point he owned three harbourside properties. Before Pad-Stein in Padstow, there was Kelly-gissey in Mevagissey! To this day we still have three ice cream parlours in the village.

Lionel Martin

Born in Nansladron House, just outside of Pentewan, Lionel Martin was the son of Edward Martin of Martin Brothers China Clay Merchants in St Austell. A wealthy family probably encouraged Lionel's love of fast cars, he sold them and raced them and then got banned for speeding. For two years he took to racing cycles, especially those at Aston Hill. When his ban was lifted, he decided to build cars, and with Robert Bamford, he founded Bamford and Martin Limited and named their first car the Aston Martin. A heritage plaque commemorating his birth can be found on Nansladron House.

WRITERS, ARTISTS & DREAMERS ALL

Mevagissey has long attracted an artistic set, it must be something in the air. On August 11th, 1906, George Bernard Shaw came to Mevagissey staying with his friends, Oswald Dickinson and Harley Granville-Barker, at Pentille House. It was intended to be a writer's retreat in order to write *The Doctor's Dilemma*. (SEE FIG. 16.)

The play discusses the efficacy and advocacy of medical treatment. A doctor has a cure for tuberculosis (TB) but can only afford to treat 1 in 5; his dilemma is who to pick. This interest in medical matters may explain why he is photographed on Polstreath Beach, our local beach, sporting an all-in-one woollen suit developed by Dr Jaeger. In 1878, a German professor named Gustav Jaeger published a book claiming that only clothing made of animal hair, such as wool, promoted health. A British accountant named Lewis Tomalin translated the book, then opened a shop selling Dr Jaeger's Sanitary Woollen System, including knitted wool union suits. These were soon called "Jaegers"; they were widely popular. (SEE FIG. 17.)

Clearly, the weather became a bit too warm for a woollen all-in-one in August, and soon Shaw and his friends stripped off and happily posed *au naturel* with only the artistic draping of a towel for the camera.

During the late 1940s, Mevagissey became a home for a variety of artists and writers. Often they lived at Heligan Mill and were referred to by the village as a commune of bohemians. (SEE FIG. 18.) They spoke of communes and a better, more Utopian way of living. Not all in the circle were so optimistic and, sadly, attempted suicides, affairs and accidental deaths were the fate of some of them. Maybe they were just unhinged dreamers, as some of the local fishermen believed. Few left such an enduring mark as architect John Archibald Campbell. The three houses at the end of Chapel Point were designed by him, and they are breathtaking examples of art deco architecture and were meant to be the forerunners of a Utopian housing project that he had submitted plans for.

Fig. 16. Pentille House where George Bernard Shaw stayed. He doesn't mention the bear but it appears to be in the grounds of Pentille House.

Fig. 17. George Bernard Shaw wearing his Jaeger and spotting a parasol. And here, George Bernard Shaw is an altogether more relaxed ensemble.

Unfortunately one evening he walked off a cliff and died. Despite this rather abrupt end Campbell clearly loved his time in the village and often referred to "Nights that pass in The Ship."

During this time the Scottish poet WS Graham was staying with the author Frank Baker on Cliff Street. In his narrative poem *The Nightfishing*, an epic ode to the fishermen of Mevagissey, "Jock" as he was predictably known, has immortalised the very lifeblood of the village. Other notables during this time included author Colin Wilson, artist John Minton, sculptor Nell Lambert, poet Peter Redgrove, potter Bernard Moss and psychologist and anthropologist John Layard.

Fig. 18. Heligan Mill, where many of the Bohemians lived. One told me that when they would walk into the village, they would sometimes be spat at by the fishermen, as they were considered so strange.

The potter, Bernard Moss is becoming very collectable, which his sons tell me would have pleased him and his wife enormously. Bernard was a Jewish German émigré who settled in Cornwall and started to produce figures in a folk art style. He moved his pottery from place to place within Mevagissey including at one time in what is now Hurley Books on Jetty Street. The British Film Institute has old pathé film reel of Bernard Moss working in his studio in Mevagissey; this was filmed near the Sunny Corner car park.

The Mevagissey air remains creative though and was once the childhood home of Ian Dury, of the Blockheads fame. Ian's Grandfather was Dr John Walker, the village GP and he built Pentillie House, up on School Hill. Ian's mother, Margaret, known as Peggy, grew up there with her two sisters and brother. They were a well-educated and upper-middle-class family. When Peggy moved to London, she met Bill Dury, who by all accounts was a working class lad with social mobility on his mind. The marriage was not successful, however. Bill resented coming home to find Peggy and her sisters chatting all night about current affairs, science and philosophy. For many stuttering marriages, the Second World War brought things to a head, and Peggy moved back to Cornwall with her son, Ian. Ian had been born in London May 12th, 1943 but was christened in St Goran Church in 1944. They lived with her mother Mary, who had moved to Penmellyn House on the Portmellon Road, her husband, Ian's grandfather, having died some years previously. For the next few years, Peggy spent her life in various locations, keeping Ian close by her. They mostly lived in London, returning to Mevagissey for holidays. In 1949 he travelled with his Aunt Molly for a fortnight's break in Mevagissey. A few days earlier, he had gone swimming at a Southend swimming pool with friends, and it was here that he contracted polio. By the time they reached Mevagissey, Ian was complaining of a terrible headache. Molly was trained in medicine and was instantly concerned, as was his grandmother, herself a doctor's wife. They called the local GP who suspected polio and sent Ian to Truro and summoned his mother from London at all haste. Ian spent the next six weeks fighting for his life having contracted a very severe form of the disease. It was clearly down to the fast reaction of the well-educated and intelligent women in his family that he survived.

SALT WATER IN THEIR VEINS

Then there are those that were tied to the water, sailor, smugglers, fishermen and boat builders.

Captain Walter Williams was a merchant seaman who sailed his boats all around the world buying and selling goods. A Mevagissey man, born in 1806, skilled and able he started by building boats, then sailing them and eventually rose to Master Mariner. An official title of great importance.

Many were dubbed smugglers, or "free traders" as they preferred to be known. William Dunn, the friend of Methodist preacher John Wesley, was well known but his father William Dunn senior was considered worse. Mevagissey boatbuilders built the fastest luggers, and so they were able to outrun the

Fig. 19. Eddie Lakeman was the last surviving fisherman of his family, a family that had fished in Mevagissey for centuries, he was also the last surviving Mevagissey lifeboatman. Roly Deighton is looking on.

customs men. Eventually, the customs men cottoned or and commissioned their own Mevagissey lugger from William Shepherd. Their new found speed soon put an end to local smuggling. The local "free traders" appalled by the boatbuilder's perfidy put him out of business in turn by never commissioning another vessel for any purpose.

Eddie Lakeman was the last surviving fisherman of his family, a family that had fished in Mevagissey for centuries, he was also the last surviving Mevagissey lifeboatman. In his own words, "When the rocket was fired, you ran, whether night or day. One Sunday afternoon, I remember, I was dressed up in my new suit when the rocket went off. The suit was ruined. Three young men in a yacht, drowned before we got there." (SEE FIG. 19.)

Percy Mitchell rose to national fame in the 1950s as an excellent boatbuilder. Working from his boatyard in Portmellon, Percy and his son Gary built over 200 boats, including those for the Admiralty, the *Windstar*, sailed by Princesses Elizabeth and Margaret and many, many fishing vessels.

FILMING IN MEVAGISSEY

The Woman He Scorned 1929

Director: Paul Czinner. Starring Pola Negri.

It has been widely reported that this was filmed in Mevagissey, but I could find no proof, so I did a little digging. I trawled through local newspapers of the day and actually found a very rare copy of the film. I can now categorically, hand on heart declare, that this was not filmed in or around Mevagissey. Great shots of Mullion, Helford, St Ives and Penzance though.

Next of Kin 1942

Made by Ealing Studios. Director: Thorold Dickinson. Starring: Mervyn Johns.

Propaganda war film by Ealing Studios. A gossipy housewife is overheard talking about what her son is doing by a Nazi spy.

I was chatting to one of the old boys in the village, and he remembers cutting school one day with a friend and heading off to the beach. To their horror, they saw a bunch of German soldiers milling about (remember this was 1942) and so the two boys armed themselves with stones and started to pelt the soldiers. I wonder what those poor actors made of their less than warm welcome?

Johnny Frenchman 1945

Made by Ealing Studios. Director: Charles Frend. Starring: Francoise Rosay, Tom Walls, Patricia Roc and Ralph Michael

Filmed almost exclusively in Mevagissey this movie is still remembered with great delight. The story tells of a feud between two fishing villages, one in Cornwall and one in France.

All scenes that are shot facing the east of the village are set in Cornwall all scenes shot facing west are the French side! Most of the village were involved as extras, and many of the older residents can point to themselves in the film, as babes in arms and their long gone parents and grandparents. This is a perfect example of how long-lived the Mevagissey community is. People come and go, but the main families stay on, the faces change a bit, but the names remain.

Never Let Me Go 1953

Made by MGM. Director: Delmer Davies. Starring: Clark Gable, Kenneth Moore, Gene Tierney, Bernard Miles and Richard Haydyn.

Philip Sutherland is an American news writer stationed in Moscow since the war; while there he falls for a Russian ballet dancer, Marya Lamarkins, who, he finds out, learned English because she fell in love with him. By all accounts, Clark Gable stayed at a local guest house and was a true gentleman.

Dracula 1979

Director: John Badham. Starring: Frank Langella (Count Dracula), Trevor Eve (Jonathan Harker), Donald Pleasance (Dr Jack Seward)

Filmed very briefly in the village. It's a "blink, and you'll miss it" moment.

Bad Education 2015

Director: Elliot Hegarty. Starring: Jack Whitehall

Oh, the village had fun with this. Once again the film crew took over the village and generally clogged up the works, but it was February so not exactly a busy time. They had wanted to shoot in August. (Can you imagine the chaos?) Local fishermen were thrilled to have their boats in the shot as they were paid a prop hire fee. Even better, for continuity, they had to also appear in the Padstow Harbour shots, and so got paid for that as well. For a cold, quiet week in winter we had a lot of fun. It's probably fair to say that whilst the village looks fantastic the Cornish are not favourably portrayed.

Various commercials most recently for Boots and Waitrose. 2014 / 2015. Nearby sites of Caerhays, Charlestown and others have also hosted scores of films. Most recently *Poldark*, *About Time* and *Miss Peregrine's Home for Peculiar Children*.

Mevagissey also turns up in fiction. It was a focal point for many of the books by EV Thompson as he used to live in the village for many years and is remembered fondly by all. The majority of his works are historical family sagas and vividly bring Mevagissey and the past to life. *The Lost Years* focuses on Heligan during its decline. Mevagissey is also the setting for the children's classic *Over Sea, Under Stone* by Susan Cooper, a mysterious supernatural thriller that starts off the *Dark is Rising* series. Lots of writers focus on this area of Cornwall, and if you'd like to read more from this area, there is a list at the back.

And of course, it has been portrayed in music and art. Mevagissey has been etched, drawn, painted and photographed over the centuries and frankly very little has changed. Confined by the sea and the landscape, Mevagissey has not been able to grow too far, and so we always recognise the village regardless of the age of the image. The harbour walls may have doubled, the houses crept up the hills, and the jetty has grown, but it's still pretty much the same. The Jetty was extended in 2015 and whilst its primary purpose is to aid the fishermen it also helps the Mevagissey Choir as they use it to give their evening quayside performances in summer. These free open air concerts are a highlight of the summer months.

TALL TALES

The following stories give a sense of local flavour. Little insights into how the village used to be, and the tales the villagers used to tell each other. We start the tales with one from a Hunkin, Roly Deighton now living in Australia. The Hunkins have lived in the village for the past 400 years and probably have a great many tales that will never see the light of day!

> *In the fifties, there was an older chap who was some sort of night watchman on the harbour. It had been a balmy summer night when my father (a driver on the Western National buses) got up just before dawn to go to work. He looked out the window and here was the old chap, fast asleep on the bench. Being still dark, the harbour was silent and calm so Dad's devilment got the better of him and he lit a leftover tuppenny-banger from Guy Fawkes Night and dropped it out of the window.*
> *The bang sent all the seagulls into a screeching frenzy - and the old man racing in ever increasing circles, looking for the 'little buggers' who had*

done it. Of course, he didn't think to look up where he would have seen the giggling face of the 'big bugger' perpetrator! Later that day, Mum and Dad were talking to a neighbour, Mrs Dollie Arthur.

She said, "Did you hear that bang this morning?"

"Yes!", said Dad, trying to look innocent, "Must have been the crack of dawn!"

That bench, where the night watchman had been sleeping, has often been at the centre of village life. (SEE FIG. 20.)

Fig. 20. Mevagissey Parliament in session. The fishermen would regularly gather on this bench and put the world to rights.

In front of our house (now Sea Sells) was a low bench seat where all the
old, retired fishermen sat to smoke and chat, reminiscing about their
seafaring days and pointing out where the young ones were going wrong. It
was known as Mevagissey Parliament. The seat was continuous and went
right across the small doorway into my Grandfather's workshop - one had
to step over it to gain entry. My father bought a motorcycle and wanted
to house it there, so grandfather (Claud Hunkin) made a flap in the seat.
Unfortunately, the old men and the Harbour Trust objected and took him
to court. Effie Hunkin was the clerk at the time, so it was Hunkin versus
Hunkin! Judge Rawlings was obviously amused by the case as he said that
he wasn't sure how the 'Parliament' was formed - whether by verbosity
or force of arms, however, he ruled that whenever access was needed,
Parliament must rise!

A case proving how stubborn fishermen can be. The Royal Navy discovered this to their cost when they lost one of their Remote Operated Vehicles (ROVs) in the 1990s. The little submarine was found bobbing about, and a local fisherman claimed it under salvage rights. When the Navy requested the return of their ROV without compensation, the submarine went "missing" until a suitable settlement was reached.

Visitors may notice a water-well tucked away by a stone staircase in a corner by St Georges Square. Was this a holy well? The source of the fatal cholera outbreak? A place where locals gather to discuss the weather? Not a bit of it, it was built in the Fifties by a local businessman. Ever looking for a way to make some more money, he touted it as a wishing well for the tourist to throw their pennies in. Protected by a metal grate and lock this enterprising businessman thought he was on to a good thing. However, he hadn't counted on the even more enterprising village children. One of the locals told me how, as a boy, he and his mates would go down to the harbour to catch fish to sell. If they came back empty handed they slipped their small bony arms through the grill and helped themselves to whatever pennies they could grab. Some children tickle trout, Meva children tickle pennies.

Tizer's Pigs.

Now here's a tale that should be told over a pint. Old man Behenna liked to sit in the local pub in the fifties and for a pound or a pint, would tell tales to the visitors, or, as they were affectionately known, the "red lips" on account of the lipstick the ladies wore. Tizer's Pigs was one such tale and whilst the names and places may be real I am quite confident that the entire tale is as tall as the Daymark on Gribbin Point.

The story starts with our narrator on his way down to the sea with his mates to go pull in his fishing nets with hopes of a large catch that he can sell.

> *"It was early in the morning, and we came down to Charlestown, and there were no nets. All the nets were gone! My Lord, he says to me, this is sum job. Then he says here! What's that thrashing out there? Oh my, that's the nets, and that's a great deal of fish. So I rows with Roger towards it to see what 'tis. But when we got there what did we see in our fishing nets but seventy great pigs! Tizer's pigs from down Pentewan have come out and weighed anchor. He looks at me and says "My son, there was 25 thousand of pilchards in those nets, and they have eaten every single one and the net anchor to boot!" "My Lord," he said, "what be us goin' to do with that now?" "Here's what I do know he says. "You two row this old moller and I get hold of that old white one by his chops, and I'll haul his head up over the stern of it. And he said all the others will follow us in."*

(Now you have to be able to picture this. We have three men in a rowing boat, probably around 16ft long. They are out at sea and surrounded by a shoal of swimming pigs that have eaten the entire catch of pilchards. One of the men is leaning out of the boat and is hauling in the largest pig, no doubt as big as the man himself and twice as fat. As he hangs onto the pig, the other two row back to shore and the shoal of pigs follow their leader.)

> *"Now boys," I says" "once we get back to Pentewan on no account must they touch the bottom. (If they could have walked out the fishermen wouldn't be able to get compensation) Now you keep 'em here whilst I go up and see*

old Tizer and settle up." Now Tizer's wife comes down to the beach and says "My husband is in an awful way, he been out all night, he lost 70 pigs." "My Lord," says Jack "We've been out an' hauled our nets, and we found a haul of pigs, not fish." So her husband's coming down the field, and he said: "That's a fine job, you got my great pigs." "That we did, we went out and got them up, we got this great one up by his chops, and we know'd the others would follow us but that a fine job they've done on our net. Every bit of our savings is now in those old pigs." And Mr Tizer said to me how many of ee be on the boat my son. Oh, we said, three of us. Well, he said you'd better have a drink, and he give us 6d.

Jack said my son, what we going buy with that 6d. And Tizer said, my son, you can have three glasses each of water!"

(I like to imagine the outrage and disgust of the teller as he got to the end of his tale and I don't doubt that as he mentioned the water, he glanced longingly at the bar and waited for someone to stand him a pint for the laugh.)

This next tale is not a tall one but gives an excellent insight into life in Mevagissey in 1919.

An extract from Tales of Harry Behenna told by Dolton Tucker's mother.

Harry joined up as a Naval apprentice in 1919 to try and earn some extra money for the family. The story takes up when Harry is coming home for shore leave.

Delighted that he would be home for Christmas he "took train" for St Austell, arriving there at ten at night. He was alone; his pals were all scattered about in various ports. The moon was shining beautifully; he would have a pleasant walk home. He felt fit. On the way down he cut a stick from a hedge, even that was company, at any rate, it was going to serve him a better purpose than he thought.

"All was well with the world until I got to "Prentice"" he said to us. (Prentice, of course, was short for London Apprentice) There he experienced a dramatic change in the weather. A black storm came in from the south-east and brought with it snow and a hurricane of wind. It lashed against him all the way. He pulled up his collar and jammed down his hat. The moon was covered with angry black clouds, he could only grope his way along. There was so much snow that he couldn't tell hedge from road. Many times he was blown against the hedge and pricked with hawthorn bushes.

Wet through, and struggling against heavy odds, his stick being his only guide along the hedges, he reached as far as the old hill, Mevagissey. There he paused, resting against a high hedge, to catch a little breath, before the final part of the journey. It must be remembered that before the new road was built, there were hedges on each side of the road, leading from the top of the old hill all along to the Vicarage Hill. After a rest he got up to the main road, travelling close to the hedge all the way. Being dark, and the wind still blowing a hurricane, his stick the only guide, he reached as far as Trewinney, opposite Vicarage Hill.

Here he put a question to himself, "shall I go down the steep and rugged vicarage hill, with its high hedges for shelter or go the School Hill way?" Without thinking more about it, he turned right and began his journey down the hill. With the high hedges and the overhanging trees, it was darker and more lonely than ever. The wind howled and whistled through the trees. A solitary owl, trying to pick up the cry of his lady pal across the valley, made matters worse by cooing "who be you, who be you" He followed Henry all the way down the hill, flying from tree to tree, sending out the same message every time "who be you, who be you, who be you." This annoyed the lonely pedestrian so much that he shouted back, "Shut up you blooming nuisance and go to sleep!"

The deep pits in the road caused by the constant use of horse and cart made Henry fall on several occasions into the muddy ruts, making himself wetter

Jetty Street, Mevagissey.

Fig. 21. A very rare image of Jetty Street. It is also possible to detect the rise in the street that protects Fore Street from an easterly surge.

*than ever. Arrived at the bottom of the hill, he proceeded along Church
Lane and down to Church Street. When he got as far as Jetty Street, he had
the feeling that he was within a few feet of home. At that moment he heard
the crunching sound of someone walking towards him. Then a flashing
light caused by a "bullseye lantern" blinded him. A voice shouted the same
message that the owl did, "Who be you, where ee from?"*

*"Before he could answer, the light shone up and down his drenched body,
when the voice shouted again, "My gosh Mr. You'm some wet; what the devil
are you doing out in this weather?" By then Henry was feeling reassured. It
wasn't a hold up for money, after all, just the jolly local bobby.*

*He told the policeman, "I've now come back from Plymouth where I've been
mobilising. You're the only thing I've seen walking all the way from station.
The worst night I've ever been in". Then he walked a few more feet to his
door at 2 a.m. footsore and weary. (SEE FIG. 21.)*

We end our stories of village life with a laugh, once more in the pub.

Fisherman's Catch.

As told to me by Gerald Cloke, another of Mevagissey's long-line families.

*"Now there was this chap that had not been fishing for too long but liked to
come into the pub at the end of the day, over a beer he would regale anyone
that cared to listen about the size of the fish he had caught that day. Sadly
he could never prove his story as the fish in question always managed to
get away. Now one day his story was even more extreme than normal, and
it finally roused an old fisherman to action. He had sat in his chair every
evening listening to the stories grow ever more outlandish until on that day
he stirred himself. "Your story is quite amazing I must say but not quite as*

amazing as mine. Whilst out fishing my line went tight, and I thought, this is a big one alright. But when I pulled it up it was not a fish at all, for I had caught an old ship's lantern and the candle was still alight inside."

The young chap laughed and said "There's no way that that's true" To which the old seadog replied, "Well you cut three feet off that sea trout, and I'll blow out the candle!"

MEVAGISSEY TODAY

Mevagissey is no longer the globally important town and port that it once was, but it is still thriving. Despite the many challenges that small communities face, especially communities where their houses are sought after by those with deeper pockets than the resident population, it continues on. The names Hunkin, Behenna (h), Cloke, Solomon, Lakeman, Bar(r)on *et al.* are littered throughout the history books as far back as they go, and are still in the village today. (SEE FIG. 22.)

The village school is full; new homes swell the roll numbers and whilst a great many houses have been bought by second home owners and used as holiday lets, the resident population remains in the majority. You only have to attend the winter events to see them well attended by all the locals. The fishing industry, despite increased competition from EU fishing vessels, has also greatly benefited from EU money and now young fishermen outnumber the old boys. It may be that tourism is now Mevagissey's primary source of revenue, but the two industries sit happily, side by side. Long may it ever be so.

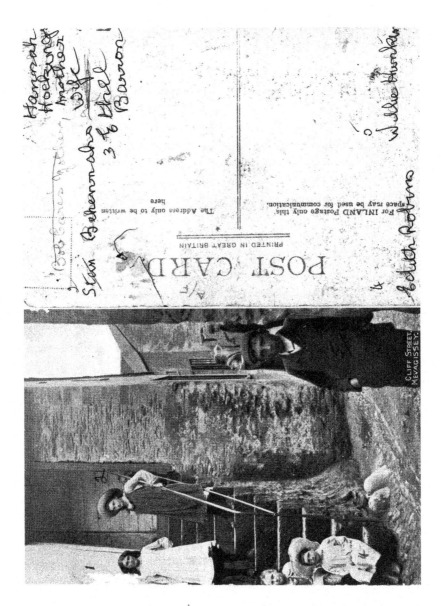

Fig. 22. The descendants of these children still live in the village today and can all point to their great-grandparents, aunts and uncles. The children in this picture are Hannah Hocking, Stan Behennah, Ethel Barron, Edith Robins and Willie Hunkin

BIBLIOGRAPHY

HAMMOND, J., *An account of St Austell. A Cornish Parish*. 1897. Skeffington.

LAKE, W., *Parochial History of the County of Cornwall*. 1870. John Camden

BIRCH, W., *Ian Dury, The Definitive Biography*. Sedgwick & Jackson

BALLS, R., *Ian Dury: Sex & Drugs & Rock 'N' Roll*. Omnibus

HITCHENS & DREW, *The History of Cornwall*. 1824. Penaluna.

BARING-GOULD, S., *The Lives of the British Saints*. 1907.

CAREW, R., *The Survey of Cornwall*. 1602. John Jagger.

HAMILTON JENKIN, A.J., *Mines and Miners of Cornwall. xiii The Lizard - Falmouth - Mevagissey*. 1967. Bradford Burton.

ROBERTS, J.K., *The Mevagissey Independents. 1625 - 1946*. 1946. The Pheonix Press.

MURRISH, R.C., *A History of the Mevagissey Methodists. 1752 - 1980*. 1980.

PINDAR, P., *The Works of Peter Pindar*. 1835. M. Walis Woodward & Co.

WESLEY J., *The Journals of John Wesley, 1735 - 1790*

FURTHER READING

Non-Fiction

(Some of these are out of print but can be found second-hand)
NEWMAN, P., *The Man Who Unleashed the Birds. Frank Baker and his circle.* 2010.
DENTON, P., *Master Mariner, Captain Walter Williams, 1806 - 1882, Of Mevagissey.* 2008. 9780954279011. Peveril Press.
DUNN, J., *Memories of Mevagissey. Meva 'Fore Now.* 2007. 9780955632303.
BEHENNA, B.A., *A Cornish Harbour.* 1995. 0952644908. Eliza Kingston Press.
DUXBURY, B., *About Mevagissey.* 1978. 090645607x. Bossiney Books.
LAKEMAN, M., *Early Tide.* Mary Lakeman.
HURLEY, L., *Scribbles from the Edge.* 2015. Mudlark's Press
HURLEY, L., *Losing it in Cornwall.* 2015. Mudlark's Press
SHEARWOOD, K., *Evening Star. The Story of a Corish Fishing Lugger.* 1970. Bradford Barton.

Fiction

COOPER, S., *Over Sea, Under Stone.* - *Young teenage adventure*
THOMPSON, E.V., *The Lost Years.* - *Family saga*
GODDARD, R., *Faultline.* - *Crime thriller*
SHERWOOD, K., *Whistle the Wind. 2nd Edition.* 2009. Kennedy & Boyd.
- *Fishing adventure*
COUBROUGH, D., *Half a pound of Tuppenny Rice.* 2016. Peter Owen. - *Crime thriller*
HARGRAVES, P., *Silent Bell.* 2012. - *The first in a historical series of nine*
KENT, L.A., *Rogue Flamingo.* 2014, Willow Orchard Pub. - *Crime adventure*

SIGN UP FOR FREE DOWNLOADS AND GREAT OFFERS

Getting to know my readers is really rewarding, I get to know more about you and enjoy your feedback, it only seems fair that you get something in return so if you sign up for my newsletter you will get a free Beach Guide to Cornwall, advance notice of new releases plus other free downloads as they get written. I don't send out many newsletters, and I will never share your details. If this sounds good, please type the following in your browser:
www.lizhurleyauthor.com

Did you enjoy this book? You can make a big difference.

Reviews are very powerful and can help me build my audience. Independent authors have a much closer relationship with their readers, and we survive and thrive with your help.

If you've enjoyed this book, then you can leave a review on Goodreads or Amazon.

ALSO BY LIZ HURLEY

Scribbles from the Edge

When everyday life is anything but every day.

Liz Hurley gathers together her newspaper columns to deliver a collection of fast, funny reads. Join in as you share the highs and lows of a bookseller, dog lover and mother in Britain's finest county. This treasure trove of little gems moves from lifestyle pieces on living day-to-day, behind the scenes in the UKs number one tourist destination, to opinion pieces on education, current affairs, science, politics and even religion. Watching the sun set over a glowing beach isn't quite so much fun when you are trying to find the keys your child hid in the sand, and the tide is coming in! Join in and discover just how hard it is to surf and look glamorous at the same time. Batten down the hatches as she lets off steam about exploding cars and rude visitors. Laugh along and agree or disagree with Liz's opinion pieces, as you discover that although life might not be greener on the other side, it's a lot of fun finding out.

Scribbles from the Edge is a lovely, light-hearted journal. It will make you laugh out loud, stop and think about larger concerns or just enjoy the beautiful descriptions of a gorgeous world as seen through her eyes.

Losing it in Cornwall

The second collection of columns from Liz Hurley, still scribbling away on the edge. Still trying to hold it together. From serious to silly her columns cover all that life throws at us. A perfect selection of little titbits, to pick up and put down or read straight through.

LOOK OUT FOR MORE GREAT BOOKS FROM MUDLARK'S PRESS COMING SOON...

Mudlark's Press

Mudlark's was established in 2015 in response to the nightmare of getting my first book published. In the end, it seemed easier to do it myself, and whilst it actually wasn't easy at all, it was fun. Coming soon are a book of walks, a guide book and a children's storybook. After that? Who knows? Maybe you have something?

Mudlark is a family nickname, and it felt nice to bring it out into the light. We have nothing to do with the Thames!